1

OFF GRID AND LOW INCOME

by

Amelia Barrett

Dedication:

To all in the Circle of Life.

May all beings benefit!

Table of Contents

INTRODUCTION

Have you seen those reality shows? You know the ones I mean: the ones where the intrepid souls live off the land, making their own way in the world? The ones that show the "self-sufficient" people?

The shows with the rugged guys and gals who make do, get by, or go without? We like these people, and we relate to them, but here's why I put "self-sufficient" in quotes: they're NOT self-sufficient! They're clever, creative, resourceful, inventive, conscientious, independent, salt-of-the-earth people, and we admire them greatly, but consider:

Most of them use a vehicle, or several vehicles, of some sort. The gator hunters, for instance, have a truck that pulls a boat trailer, that hauls their boat. Some of them have, or borrow, ATVs. The folks in the frozen north use a farm tractor. They use guns. They use saddles. They wear store-bought clothes, and (most of them) wear store-bought footwear. Most of them take themselves and their critters to doctors, chiropractors, vets, and (the ones who still have their teeth), dentists.

Without a rubber plantation and a tire factory, they can't make their own tires. Without a garage and fabricating machines for building and fixing vehicles, they can't build cars, trucks, tractors, etc. Without a textile mill for their fabrics and a tannery for their leather goods, they are no more self-sufficient than any city dweller.

And; that's okay.

So long as you're not thinking that going off grid is going to allow you to cut all ties with civilization, we're good. (Of course, your ambition may be to go the total mountain man route, if so, I have nothing to offer you. I consider such an approach extreme, unbalanced, and unnecessary, akin to throwing out the baby with the bath water. Civilization sucks in a lot of ways, but it has some good stuff, too).

If you're simply wondering if you could make a go of living off grid, and what, exactly, doing so is all about, this book is for you. I call it "Off Grid and Low Income" because I intend it for people like we were; my partner and I. We went off grid to try to keep some options open, faced with living in poverty, and seeing the ability to work full time receding in the rear view mirror. When we left the city behind, one of us was on disability, and the other, a wage slave: both our incomes combined were never going to allow us to buy into the American dream. Neither of us had a pension plan, other than Social Security. So many companies have looted their employee pension plans – and continue to do so – it was probably just as well. My partner had run a small business most of his adult life; I had moved from one "good job" (an oxymoron, in my opinion), to another, without finding anything like security. As the years went by and the parasitic rich became ever richer and more parasitic, it became obvious to both of us that the gravy train had left the station without us, and wasn't due back any time soon.

With our "golden" years bearing down on us, we found ourselves faced with choosing between poverty, and **abject** poverty. We had a bit of help, but most of what's in this book we learned as we went. Here's hoping our experience will give you, and point you to, advantages we didn't have.

CHAPTER 1: No Rent, No Mortgage, What's Not to Love?

Sounds great, doesn't it? Your own little piece of paradise, free and clear (you know...once it's paid for). No utilities, no bill for this, no dues for that.

Well, guess again: where we live, there are no wells (think rocks: lots of them, lots of BIG ones), so we haul water, which means we have a water bill. We have cell phones, and we have the bill for those. We have Internet coverage, so as to be informed and to be able to shop without extra miles traveled, so we pay for that. There's no broadcast TV that we can get from here, so we pay for satellite TV (no; not a necessity, but relatively cheap entertainment). Reception is horrible for the over-the-air radio stations we can get out here, so we have bills for our satellite radios. We've taken out loans for one thing and another over the years, so we pay for those.

Living in the back of beyond, and obliged to drive heavy, older vehicles that can pull the water trailer, and that get few miles per gallon, we pay more for fuel than we would if we didn't need so much mechanical muscle. Luckily, my partner is a retired mechanic, and can work on the things, or we would have to pay shop repair rates, instead of just buying the parts.

Those rocks I mentioned are hell on boots and shoes, so we go through a lot of those. If you can't afford the best quality (and you don't dare buy the crappiest/cheapest), you spend a fair amount on footwear. I like a particular brand of jeans, so I treat myself to new jeans from time to time (they're not that expensive, and the fit is reliable and comfortable), but my friend gets his secondhand. We buy new undies and socks: everything else; shirts, jackets, sweaters, comes from thrift stores.

In addition to being on Social Security, we're what's known in some circles as "horse poor." We have, through purchase, adoption, gifts (and in one case, dumping by a "friend"), acquired five horses and one club-footed mule. We're able to keep them healthy by feeding them bermuda grass hay and crimped oats (no fancy designer feeds), and by not exposing them to other people's horses, as happens at boarding stables, where they would be exposed to diseases and parasites.

Those rocks do us one huge favor: we turn our horses out after morning feeding time to meander around the Forty, and thanks to the rocks, their hoofs wear naturally. This eliminates the need for a farrier to trim and/or shoe them. If we needed a farrier every six weeks for six equines, we couldn't do it. My friend occasionally rasps a chip smooth, and that's all the hoof care they need. Being able to ramble all day keeps the one riding horse (the others aren't trained) happy and content. Furthermore, that horse is just as peaceful and agreeable after months of no riding as he would be if ridden every day, because he's never cooped up in a pen or stall getting antsy.

Why do we have so many horses, when their feed and supplies take about a third of our combined income? A friend who ran a food bank was wondering that. My then-husband asked her, "Didn't you start the food bank as your way of doing good works?" She agreed that that was the case. He waved his arm at our animals and said, "Well; this is our way of doing good works." (She understood: I'm sure plenty of people don't, but the hell with 'em).

So, anyway; there are kinds and degrees and causes of being "poor," and more and more people, some of whom never used to consider themselves economically challenged, are bumping their noses up against the reality of not-enough. Never quite enough, no matter how hard they work, no matter how many hours they put in, no matter what choices they make or what roads they take. The take-away from all this is: if you're thinking if you can just get your hands on a piece of land and build yourself a homestead, your money worries will be over, well...hold that thought and keep reading!

* * *

As this is written (2014), being "poor" involves making $11,670 for an individual, adjusted upward modestly for additional members of the household. For example; the poverty level for a family/household of 4 is $23,850. When I worked at Legal Aid years ago, we accepted as clients anyone making up to the federally-defined poverty level, plus 25%. I would consider that "+25%" to be "low-income," although if you're in that bracket, you probably feel just plain <u>poor</u>! Income disparity in this country is shameful, and I don't know what it's going to take to bring things back into line. When so many of the voices demanding that people "pull themselves up by their own bootstraps" are working tirelessly to make sure nobody has boots, it's hard to imagine how people are expected to do that.

Entry into the middle class was supposed to be assured for anyone who was willing to work hard and save their money. Part of that middle class dream included home ownership. Today, too few think in terms of "home." The ones that can afford to buy a house think in terms of exactly that: a house, a commodity, to be "flipped" - at a profit, of course, for what else is there, but money?

Given that we Americans have created a culture of greed, greed, greed, one is obliged to put one's hands on a certain amount of money, as a practical matter. The Supreme Court has declared that money = speech, but if that equation were valid, speech would also equal money, and it doesn't. If you don't believe me, try this simple experiment: Next time the cupboard is bare, go to the store, load up your cart, and have a nice chat with the checker in lieu of paying. I predict that you will leave there without your food.

If you're reading this, though, chances are you don't need to try the experiment. You already feel the pinch of this economy. The point isn't whether you technically qualify as "poor" or "low-income" according to some official standard. The point is: do you have enough money to pursue your dreams, or if not that, to meet your basic needs?

Assuming that one of your dreams is to leave the city and "live off the land," on your own little homestead, it can be done. What's needed is what poor folks have always been good at: improvising. Unless you're newly poor, I don't have to tell you that. If you are newly poor, you'll catch on quick.

If you're on Social Security or disability, you don't have much money, but you also don't have to drive every day, so that's actually an advantage. It helps not having to commute, because most land that poor people can afford is pretty far off the beaten path. If you're still employed, you will have to consider that. When we bought this place, I was still working. I traveled 125 miles a day, all told, and my first and last two miles were over unmaintained county roads. Dirt roads at the best of times, mud bogs or ice fields at the worst. We don't always need four wheel drive, but we always have to have good ground clearance. The times I figured out I did need four wheel drive, I was dressed for the office, not for slogging around in the mud, locking hubs, so I was occasionally a very vexed commuter! Nothing as old as our rides came with all-wheel-drive, and traction control relies solely on the driver's ability and judgment, with no help from the vehicle's onboard computer!

A neighbor where we lived when we first went off grid moved out into the boonies with his beloved little sports car. By the time we met him, he had switched to an old pick up, and the pretty little sports car was a hostel for chipmunks and pack rats.

13

That's probably the first adjustment you'll have to make; having your choice of wheels dictated by what works for your new environment, rather than by what blows your hair back. We didn't mind too much. We love sports cars, too, but being horse people, trucks have always been part of our lives, and we also love them. Being that neither of us has to commute these days, low miles per gallon isn't the make-or-break proposition it used to be. When you get paid once a month, by which time you're out of **everything**, you need a surefooted ride that has lots carrying capacity, in order to re-provision in one haul. Any trips we make later in the month, to check the mail, etc., are so few and far between, we just don't spend as much on gas as we would if obliged to drive daily.

The other thing to keep in mind if you do have to commute, is the time. I know there are people who commute 2 or 3 hours each way between their work and home, which is hard for me to imagine. Most of them (I sincerely hope!) live in places where a lot of that commuting is to get to and from public transportation, not driving the whole way. In my case, an hour-and-a-half of driving each way was enough to have me constantly battling to keep from falling asleep at the wheel. In the morning, it was because I was forced to get up way before I was ready, and in the afternoon, because I was worn out from my day.

My partner would sometimes call me before I left work and ask me to stop for something "on the way home." He used to get some snarky responses to these requests. After an hour-and-a-half drive in, 8 hours on the (stressful) job, and facing an hour-and-a-half drive home, I had little energy and left and zero enthusiasm for any little side trips. I made the extra stops, but I hated feeling obligated to do it, and I hated him for asking. Of course, it made no sense to think he should drive all the way into town when I was already there, but I was there stressed out, worn out, and not prepared to go above and beyond. Therefore, consider the affect on your relationship, if any, of moving out to the back of beyond with a full time worker/commuter in the mix.

The last two years that I was employed, I received two raises. Both times, I ended up losing ground financially. Each year, the premium for my employer-provided health insurance went up, and the price of gas went up, and those two things ate up my pay increase and then some. That's another thing: if you're employed and moving out in the country depends on that income, can you expect it to be there for the foreseeable future?

If you're employed, is there someone who will keep the home fires burning? I never got stranded in town, as might well have happened, due to winter weather and road closures. If I had, our animals would still have had my partner at home to care for them. If you have no partner, or if both of you are employed, you must find someone dependable to call upon if you are prevented from getting home for twenty-four hours or more. Moving far from friends and family, and into territory where you don't know anyone makes this problematic.

So; yes, there are still bills and expenses, and there are still stressors, even in (mostly) leaving the rat race behind. That's not to say it can't be done, but there are some things to think about.

CHAPTER 2: Getting Land Without Enough Money

<u>Outright Purchase</u>

My then husband/now friend (long story) and I bought a house in the early nineties when we were both employed full-time. Long before the Bush economic debacle of 2008, we found ourselves in trouble. He lost his job, by which time I had quit my full time job and started a little bookkeeping and record keeping business, working from home. When he got laid off, the income from that little side business wasn't enough to keep us afloat, and we soon got behind in our mortgage.

In order to buy in the first place, we'd had to borrow the down payment from a friend of a friend. He was holding a second mortgage for his money, which turned out to be fine and dandy, because he was a realtor. When he found out we were facing foreclosure, and not wanting to lose out on his investment, he listed the house. It was a nice house, and, as I mentioned, the market hadn't tanked, so before long, we had a buyer. That was excellent news for him, as he recovered his investment, and it was pretty good news for us, because we ended up with a few thousand of our own. I say "pretty good," because I really loved that house, but too bad for me.

We loaded what would fit into the old school bus my spouse had converted into a motor home, and in which we had lived before we got our real home. What didn't fit went into storage. (Most of that, we ended up losing, as time went by and no suitable dwelling came our way). I had only had two homes in my life: the one where my parents lived when I was born, and the one we'd just lost, so, as you can imagine, I was not a happy camper, no pun intended. After my parents divorced, first my mother, and then my first husband dragged me from pillar to post. A lifetime of living in rentals, and having to go hat-in-hand to a landlord/landlady and ask pretty please could we have a dog, could we paint the living room—if we bought the paint!--and being told NO!, and let's just say I had a very sour taste in my mouth about renting.

I told my husband: no rent and no mortgage hanging over my head, EVER AGAIN!!!! We started casting about for land, where we planned to build.   (Thus far, we've/I've been stuck in trailers, but at least, there is no mortgage, my trailer is mine, and I do still hope to build someday).

So; we had a few thousand dollars with which we were able to buy six acres of land. The acres were separate parcels, but they were adjoining, so we could spread out. We could also sell two off when the money ran out. That happened pretty quickly, when we were obliged to put in a septic system rather than using a composting toilet and a grey water system. That septic system set us back $4000. (Only a few years later, when we bought the forty acre parcel we live on now, and the same size septic system cost us $10,000)!

By the way, that septic system led to our being robbed. The guy that put in the system called and asked if we wanted the piles of dirt left from installing the septic tank. We planned to use that dirt for raised bed gardening, and told him yes; we wanted the dirt. Whereupon, he came onto our land when we were away and hauled off our dirt. That was the first time we were victimized, but far from the last, or even the worst case. But, being low-income, we didn't have the time and/or money for legal assistance, and it was only dirt, so we didn't pursue our rights, which guys like that count on.

Very long story short: we lived on our four acres as comfortably as we could for several years. The comfort level at first varied directly with the condition of the roads: I was commuting to a job in the city, and the winters here in northern Arizona can be intense. As I mentioned, nowadays, many vehicles have all wheel drive standard, but nothing we could afford offered us that. We ended up with a Suzuki Samurai, which had four wheel drive and great fuel economy, but wasn't insulated worth a damn. That was some cold driving, but at the time, I was just glad to be able to get back and forth, no matter the weather.

Then, partially because it was near a state highway and access wasn't too difficult, the parcels around us began to sell. People who were **not** poor or low-income, and who didn't want poor or low income neighbors, began surrounding us. There were also people **we** didn't want as neighbors, regardless of their income level. Like; the people whose dog came onto our land and killed two of our cats because the asshole owners flouted the leash law. Four acres was no longer enough to make us feel that we could live in peace, so we put three of them up for sale. Once we got enough money from them to purchase the "forty" that we live on now, we sold the remaining acre, moved here and started over yet again.

Therefore; if you own something big that you can sell for enough money to buy your land outright, that's one option, and there are others.

Assuming Payments

In this economy, a lot of people are going under. Some are interested enough in protecting their credit rating to simply let you take over their payments. If you find a deal like this, be careful. Don't agree to anything on a handshake! Insist that everything be put in writing, and then, have a lawyer review it. Even if you can't qualify for Legal Aid, or if they don't take this type of case, they may be able to refer you to someone who can help. Many attorneys offer a free or low-cost consultation. They won't give you a lot of time, so be prepared. Take your contract, a copy of the seller's mortgage, and a list of any questions you may have. Take notes! If the lawyer warns you off, you can either decline to sign, or ask the property owner to modify the contract so you're better protected. If he/she is on the up-and-up, they won't kick too hard about this. If they refuse, or try to push you into signing, by threatening to sell to somebody else, etc., leave. You're offering to do them a favor: if they start throwing their weight around, something isn't right.

Seller Carry-back

Sometimes, a seller isn't in trouble, but doesn't want the hassle of going through realtors or whatever. If that's the case, and they simply want to handle things themselves in order to save money, that's fine, but my advice is the same as before: run it by a lawyer. You need some things spelled out, like: what day of the month your payment is due, and how long a grace period you have, if any, before you incur late payment penalties. You want to know how much interest you're paying, how much of your payment applies to the interest, and how much to the principle. A lawyer will help you wade through all this.

As in the first example if the seller tries to pressure you, or objects to your caution in having an attorney review the pertinent documents, find another piece of land.

If a seller wants a down payment, you may be able to negotiate that, too. You might offer to make higher payments for so many years until the down payment is covered, and then drop down to the regular monthly payment amount to pay off the balance.

If the seller insists on cash for the down payment, ask if he/she wants the money for something specific. It could be that they want to buy something, and you could finagle a trade for that item, which they would then accept in lieu of the money. A friend of mine knew a guy who bought houses for no money down that way. One seller wanted a nice travel trailer, and the guy did a trade of something he had for such a trailer, and persuaded the seller to accept that as his down payment.

Barter

Perhaps you have a skill a seller would be interested in: plenty of folks have found out that their skills aren't enough to get them out of the unemployment lines, but those skills are still worth something. It could be that there's some land owner somewhere that needs to get a project done, but lacks the money to pay someone to do it. They might be interested in getting that project done in exchange for a down payment.

Whatever arrangement you come to, <u>get it in writing</u>. Do it up front, too: don't do their work for them, only to be left with nothing to show for it. If a seller balks at operating on the up and up, it could mean they're not. Walk away, and keep looking.

Be imaginative and resourceful, keep your eyes and ears open, and you may well think up or hear of some way to buy land without money up front. Just be realistic about what you can afford to pay each month, or you could end up in trouble later on. Don't do a deal if following through is going to depend on winning the lottery!

Tax Sales

I knew a group of people who purchased land from tax defaulters. Here (I don't know how it may be where you live), the County Treasurer conducts a sale of such properties every February. You can get a list of parcels where the owner has defaulted on their taxes. You pay the back taxes and notify the owner by certified mail, return receipt requested, that you have done so. You give them a certain amount of time, set by law, to repay you. If they don't, you become the owner of the land. Again; how this is done can, and probably does, vary from one locale to another, so you will need to research this for the area that interests you. My friends who did this said most of the time, when they get that notice, the owners figure out some way to pay that debt and keep title to their land. There are others, though, who can't/won't/don't, and you've bought yourself a piece of land for the back taxes. In the case of very rural property, that can be a few hundred bucks.

Whether the person paying the tax is entitled to interest or other monies in addition to the taxes paid may (and probably does) vary from state to state. Another good reason to go for a consultation with an attorney. And remember: go prepared with questions, and take notes. When you're dealing with a lawyer, never forget that time is money!

99-Year Lease

I've heard of someone going the 99-year lease route - in Mexico. This was back when the Mexican government was "nationalizing" properties belonging to foreigners, that is; taking it away from them. This one party got around that by securing a 99-year lease of some acreage belonging to one of the Native American tribes down there. Since the tribes there have sovereignty, as they do here, there was nothing the Mexican government could do about it. The Americano in question wasn't planning to live another 99 years, and so wasn't worried about what he would do when the lease ran out!

I mention it here not knowing if it's at all feasible, possible, or practical to think in terms of doing such a thing in this country. I simply want to encourage you to leave no stone unturned (no pun intended) when it comes to securing that plot of ground where you can live as independently as possible, even without the money to do so in conventional terms.

CHAPTER 3: The Roof Over Your Head

If you're poor, as I assume you are, since you're reading this, you're most likely not buying a house and land, just raw land. That means you'll need to start with the very basic requirements: a driveway/road, and a septic system. The same guy can probably both grade your drive, and install the septic system. That's going to be a big upfront expense, unless you can live without it (the septic system, not the driveway). You might be able to get onto and off of your land without having a driveway graded, but you aren't going to be allowed to live there without some means of proper human waste disposal. In some areas, you can have an out house, if that suits you. Personally, I've encountered enough daddy longlegs to last me, and for some reason, they **really** like outhouses. Nor are they the only critters you might encounter there. It's up to you: if the regs permit it, and that's really the way you want to go, have at it.

A note about septic systems; they're alive! A septic system works because of the microorganisms in it that break down human waste. If these are killed off, your septic system will stop working, and may back up into the house! If you have a septic system, you have to get into the habit of checking things like toilet paper, detergents, etc., to make sure they're safe for septic systems. Something that isn't: chlorine bleach, which definitely kills the friendly bugs that your system depends on.

As far as what kind of dwelling you're going to live in, the options for a poor person are pretty much limited to building a kit home, building from scratch, or getting a mobile/modular. Look into the requirements for minimum square footage, length of a trailer, etc., in your location. If you're building from your own ideas, get your drawings re-done by an architect or an engineer so they will meet code.

You are going to find that the regs spell everything out. We know of two cases where owners bought acreage and parked a travel trailer on it in which to live. Both were disgusted to learn than in their chosen county, a travel trailer can only be on the property for 90 days in a calendar year.

And another thing: there will be **mud**. If you're lived in the city all your life, where everything is paved, you have never encountered mud like the mud that will confront you in the country.

If you're building your own, I strongly urge the inclusion of a mud room, preferably with running water. This will give you a space for removing and cleaning mucky boots - and wiping down paws so your dog can accompany you into the main part of the dwelling, dogs being family, after all.

If building a mud room won't be an option, do the next best thing. Mark out a space adjoining the entrance, and fill it in with gravel, cinders, or sawdust. Cover this area, or part of it, with an awning if possible, to shelter under while you clean up. You'll want a couple of good heavy boot scrapers, too.

Inside, if you don't have wall-to-wall carpeting, don't bother. If your dwelling came with it, think about ripping it out. We had a friend who installed carpeting, and he wouldn't have the stuff in his own house. As he told us, "Two guys can carry in a roll of new carpet, but it takes four or more guys to carry that carpet out. There's only one way a carpet gains weight." (I know; *eeuwww*, right)?

Carpeting is a haven and refuge for dirt, dust mites, flea eggs, and bacteria. My ex used to sell vacuum cleaners. Sometimes a homeowner would schedule two salesmen to come out on the same day. He loved being the <u>second</u> guy to demo his machine. He would go in right after the first guy, vacuum the same place his competitor had just finished, and show the homeowner how inferior the first machine had been. Was the first machine inferior? Well, usually; as my ex sold a <u>very</u> good vacuum, but, in fact, there's always dirt in a carpet, if anybody lives in the house!

We had another friend, who vacuumed every single day, but she'd never steam cleaned her carpets. She put her house up for sale and decided she wanted to steam clean to get the place ready to show. She was shocked to find that her "tan" carpet was actually ivory! She and her family had been living with a nasty carpet, and her daily vacuuming hadn't put a dent in the filth.

Much better are rugs that can be snapped up and tossed in the washing machine. Dirt is one thing, but; ick. (If the idea of no carpeting seems too harsh for bare feet, there's a solution for that, too: don't go barefoot. Learn to love you some fluffy slippers).

CHAPTER 4: Let There Be Lights

If your land was cheap, as ours was, it's probably not near power lines. Do you need electricity? We started out without it. You may want to rough it to the extent that you won't need electricity at all, but for us that was never going to be our permanent lifestyle.

The Internet wasn't available at our off grid place, but then I was working full time, and I could use the computer at work for personal stuff at lunch, or before and after hours. Had we had any of the sites listed in Resources, below, life would have been a lot easier. Early on, I found several small loom designs I could build for myself, and the 'Net continues to be a great resource. (Recently, I even found a way to re-string and re-tune my guitar to make it as user friendly as a mountain dulcimer)!

Anyway; at home, it wasn't absolutely critical to have a solar setup first thing, so we made do with battery-powered lights, candles, and kerosene lamps. (We also bought a wind-up alarm clock, so I could get up in time for my daily commute without depending on battery power).

That's fun; getting up in the dark a good part of the year and trying to dress, do my hair and put on a little makeup by candlelight or flashlight! Knowing I was about to head out into the dark, especially on days with snow falling and the roads icy – once I got to anything recognizable as a "road" - made me wonder how my life had come to such a pass. If you have to drag yourself out of a cozy bed on a nasty winter morning while your partner snores on, it's hard not to be resentful!

I stopped on the way to work for coffee; it's a good idea to break up an hour-and-a-half commute, in my experience. Besides; making coffee at home would have meant leaving my toasty bed even earlier. The lure of caffeine lacked enough leverage to pry me out from under those cozy covers even a minute early. Yeah; in case it hasn't occurred to you, no power means no automatic coffee maker to incentivise your awakening. We didn't have a problem with using an old fashioned coffee pot, but trying to <u>find</u> one was a challenge. We found a nice big stainless steel one – in the camping department! 'Cause, you know; no one makes coffee on top of the stove anymore, right? And you can pretty much forget finding filters for a percolator. They're all made for the brewing baskets of those automatic coffee makers. So; you punch a hole in the filters you can get (to accommodate the center pipe) and use those.

I have since acquired (from thrift stores) a couple of glass coffeepots with plastic thingies that use cone filters. To make coffee in those, you heat your water in the tea kettle and pour it over the grounds in the cone. If you want a full pot, it usually takes two or three pours, so it isn't that convenient, but if you're puttering around the kitchen anyway, it's just a matter of remembering to check and see if there's room in the cone for more water.

Nowadays, I use a French press to <u>cold</u> brew a strong coffee concentrate, in anywhere from four hours to overnight. This will keep under refrigeration for several days. I put two ounces of concentrate in my tall mug and top it up with hot water. Makes for a coffee that is very tasty, and easier on my digestion than the harsh, hot-brewed stuff, so I'd make my coffee this way even if I lived in town.

Kerosene lamps sound romantic, don't they? My dad was a railroad man from the early days, and when I found a couple of old-fashioned-looking red kerosene lanterns, I bought two of them. Let me tell you: we tried every brand of "odorless" lamp fuel we could find and they all <u>stank</u>. It didn't bother me as much as the smell of gasoline does, thank goodness, but, ick. Not only that; if you have cats and dogs – and sometimes-clumsy humans – in the household, candles and kerosene lamps must be used with caution! I highly recommend that candles and kerosene lamps only be employed if they're hung from brackets or placed in wall sconces. Even that's a nuisance, if your dwelling is small; it's easy to turn to reach for something, and bump your head on a lantern. And then there's the fact that, unless you can spring for the most expensive, state-of-the-art kerosene lamps – and there are some, but they're not cheap – they suck as a light source. If Abraham Lincoln really did study his law books by kerosene lamp light, that right there is enough to elevate him to hero status in my book.

Recently, I've discovered some nice solar-powered lanterns. One kind can even be charged using a USB port if the day is cloudy. Some have better waterproofing than others; good to know if it starts to rain after you hang your lantern outside to charge. Check these out; they may save you a lot of money on batteries.

It's depressing, not to have enough light. I've long felt that I have Seasonal Affective Disorder. It's no mystery to me that people in far northern latitudes kill themselves at an alarming rate, I kid you not. My continued existence is due entirely to some kind of stubbornness gene, because I was not happy living without adequate light.

As if that weren't bad enough; without electricity to run the pump, we didn't have running water. Living without proper lighting is one thing. Living without running water was too much to ask.

When we found out one of our neighbors planned to sell out and move back to town; we beat it over to his place and made a deal for his solar panels! He only had a small array, and a few batteries, but it was enough to let us have electric lights in the evening – and a pump for running water. (We also had lousy TV again).

We have more panels today, and more batteries, although still not enough to have power 24/7. Much to our dismay, we found out that batteries that go into service together, fail together. We had one go bad a couple of years ago, then another one, and pretty soon, we didn't have enough batteries to do anything. We couldn't run our lights and TV even for the few hours we employ them, between six and ten p.m. My friend sold a truckload of scrap metal, and we were able to buy three replacement batteries from the proceeds: six more would have been closer to what we need. Most days, assuming plenty of sunlight during the day, that's enough for us to get through the evening. I try to confine my use of the computer to the daytime. The battery charges up the evening before, allowing me about an hour and a half of work time. If I need to use the printer, I either wait until evening, or I run the inverter long enough for the job I'm doing.

If you're not up to speed on installing and using solar power systems, you either want to educate yourself about them or accept that you will have to pay someone to set up, maintain, and repair yours. If you have to call an electrician, be prepared to pay a "trip charge" for having him come out to your place. And, speaking of electricians; they don't all know about solar set ups, so that will also limit who you can turn to for help. The place where you buy your panels may be able to help you find someone who can help you with these things.

For us, using the blender, running the washing machine or the vacuum cleaner, requires the generator, as our solar setup just isn't big enough. We try to schedule those things for the same day to save on gas. If there are a lot of cloudy days, making it necessary to use the generator in the evening, we often run out of gas for the generator between paydays. So; we don't use the blender or the vacuum cleaner at all after that point. Any clothes we can't wait to use, we wash by hand.

I bought two clean five-gallon buckets just for laundry (one each for washing and rinsing), and a washer gizmo that looks like a bathroom plunger, except that the business end is made of rigid plastic. It forces water and soap through the clothes, and it uses muscle power, so there's no fuel or electricity needed. Does a hell of a job, too. Between it and the washing machine, I only need to haul bedding to town, where a couple of laundromats have triple loaders. Believe me; if I could figure out how to 1) get my hands on my own triple loader and 2) magic up the power to run the thing (not sure even our generator could handle it), the laundromat would be history. I enjoy going there about as much as a trip to the dentist.

Luckily for us, in our part of the state, the sun shines most days. The days when it doesn't, we could sure use a wind generator. We have plenty of wind, whether the sun is shining or not. We don't have one because the commercially available ones cost more than we can afford. We haven't built our own, in spite of my friend's mechanical abilities, because he appears not to want one as badly as I do!That being the case, this is one subject I can't tell you much about.

I have learned that the VAWT configuration (it stands for Vertical Axis Wind Turbine) is supposed to be better than the propeller-types. The latter have to have a brake, or they will tear themselves apart in a high wind. A VAWT just keeps going faster. I don't know why the power companies only seem to use the propeller-type, but it seems like the VAWT design works better for the DIY crowd, if all the Youtube videos are any indication. Check them out, and maybe you can add this to your power set-up.

CHAPTER 5: Warmth

If you're lucky enough to live in an area where you won't need to heat your home in the winter, you can skip this part. It's likely, however, that you will need to give the matter some thought. I've lived in Arizona much of my life, and even in the desert areas, it gets cold at night. I don't know about the Southeastern states, but I can imagine that even in the swamps, the nights can be cool and damp enough to make some kind of heating desirable, if only to dry the air inside your home.

Electric

You're poor, you expect your handful of solar panels to provide enough juice to run space heaters, maybe even a whole house electric furnace. HAHAHAHAHAHAHAHA!

Seriously; NOT GOING TO HAPPEN. If you have the money for that kind of set up, you are not poor, by anybody's reckoning!

Propane/butane/bottled gas

At this writing, in 2014, propane is right at $4 a gallon and expected to go higher. In some parts of the country, even if you have a tank that will hold more, you are limited to 100 gallons. If you only use propane to run your water heater, a small RV-type propane fridge, and do a little cooking, you can probably get by with a tank small enough to put in your vehicle and take to one of those places that will fill it for you. In that case, the cost of propane may be painful, but livable.

On the other hand, if you heat your home with propane, and you have a big tank that they come out and fill, you're going to pay – if you can - until it hurts. As I said; there are parts of the countrywhere the companies that sell propane are rationing the stuff. If you need that gas to heat your home, that can hurt, too. I know a man who lived in central Arizona who was cold all winter, for two years in a row, because he couldn't afford the propane to heat his small house – and that was years ago, before the price went up and the availability went down.

It doesn't help that, apparently, there's no shortage of propane. If what I've heard is true, the companies are selling it off to other countries that can pay more for it. That's all well and good, from a dollars-and-cents, business standpoint, but some people think the moral issue is just as important. You know; the idea that first, we should be taking care of our neighbors here at home. Just sayin'.

Wood

First of all, check the darn regs. In some areas, and it may not be statewide, wood stoves are prohibited. When they're not prohibited, there can still be requirements as to what kind of stove you can use. I read about one that I'd love to get, that burns 12 hours on an armful of wood. Having spent several years now, spending what seems like every spare moment trying to get our hands on enough wood for our stoves each winter, it sounds too good to be true. Well, for us, it is: The one I mentioned that's so efficient sells for $4000. That's my Social Security for several months. As you may imagine, I don't have that much discretion in my "discretionary spending." I must resign myself to being up several times a night to tend to my stove, and to having a good portion of my tiny living room devoted to wood storage. I pay for those rare times when I wake up and say, "The hell with it," roll over and go back to sleep. Those times mean I get up in the morning, put on long underwear, boot socks, sweats, fleece booties, my robe, and a hoodie, until I can get the stove cranking again. After it's gone cold like that, it takes a good hour before the place warms up enough to peel off all the layers and hurry into that day's clothes. Not fun.

We bought my stove second hand and installed it ourselves. The pipe had to go out through the wall, instead of straight up and through the ceiling. It didn't draw very well, but it seemed to work okay, and it was what it was. Then one afternoon I woke up from a nap to find my little dwelling full of smoke. Something about the winds that day overcame my stove pipe's ability to draw, and the smoke took the path of least resistance back into the house. I have asthma: I was able to get up and get out of there without having an attack, but it freaked me out.

I got on my trusty Internet to do some research (perhaps you will say I should have done that to begin with, but who knew)? Lo and behold, it turns out that, if you have to go out through the wall instead of the ceiling with your stove pipe, it's better to have two forty-five degree bends than one ninety-degree bend. The pipe will draw better. You can believe I bought those extra pipe joints ASAP!

We also had to change the baffle inside the stove, to re-direct the smoke and improve the draw. If you're not mechanically inclined, get somebody to help that knows about stoves. Barter for something they need or help with a project of theirs; you know the drill.

So; given that you have to have a good stove – they're not created equal – and you have to know how to run the pipe, what's wrong with heating with wood? I mentioned that thing about disturbed sleep, but we'll chalk that up to not having the money for a modern, super-efficient stove. Maybe you can luck into one of those, and your winter nights' sleep will be unbroken.

There's still the matter of firewood. The price of firewood varies from season to season, and according to the type of wood that's available. The best load of firewood I ever got was mixed juniper (common in this area) and aspen, with just a little bit of pine. I started my fires with pine, loaded up the stove with juniper, and put a piece of two of aspen in last. The pine is pitchy, so fairly easy to get going. The juniper burns pretty steadily, and the aspen burns hot with a pleasant popping sound. In all the years I've been heating with wood, I've had only that one nice mixed load. You get what you can afford, and what they bring you.

Wood bought in the spring and early summer is cheapest; that bought at the end of summer costs more, and during the winter? Forget it: you're going to pay bigtime for firewood you buy in the winter. For one thing, the seller doesn't have that much left, and for another, he knows you're in a bind. That being the case, do what you can to get your wood by midsummer at the latest.

How much? Can't help you there. It depends on your stove, how warm you need to keep the house (as when there are elders or babies to consider), how well the house holds heat, and how cold your winters are. After the first winter or two, you'll have a better idea. The first year, lay in as big a wood supply as you think you'll need, and then get some more, if you can afford it.

If you have a truck, or a car that gets around okay off road and can pull a trailer, and you have a chain saw, check with the Forest Service about a wood cutting permit. These are typically much cheaper than buying firewood pre-cut. (If you've never cut firewood before, you'll soon figure out why the stuff commands the prices it does).

If you've never used a chainsaw, get someone to show you what to do. If not, you could be trading your cheap firewood for a horrible accident. One thing I can tell you: when you're holding the saw, you use one hand to operate the trigger, and the other forward, to support and guide the saw: be sure to keep the arm that supports the saw straight, not with the elbow bent. If you bend that elbow and the saw "kicks," you'll pull it right into your face.

I know that because I lived in Charlotte, North Carolina when

Hurricane Hugo hit, taking down an enormous number of trees. People who had never touched a chainsaw were buying them to clear away the mess; the emergency rooms were seeing so many injuries among these amateurs, that they did a public service announcement about it.

One year, we got a wood cutting permit, and spent absolutely every free weekend for months out in the forest cutting wood. The first couple of weekends, it was kind of fun; I like camping, and I like picnics. By the third weekend, with who knew how many to come exactly like it, I was SO ready to forget the whole thing....

Near where we live now, there's someone that sometimes takes out trees to make room to extend his fencing. Neither he nor any of his friends heats with wood, so he's been kind enough to alert us when these trees come available. We go out and haul them home to cut up for firewood. What we'll do when he no longer needs room for more fences, I don't like to think about.

The other thing I dislike about firewood is having it in my house. Firewood is dirty. You can't carry it in without little bits of bark and dirt falling off. And, it brings hitchhikers. I woke up one night with a spider in my ear canal – I didn't know it was a spider, just that something was scrabbling around in there! I managed to tamp down my panic enough to grab a flashlight and shine it into my ear. I was leaning over the sink, and when the critter emerged, I brushed it off flushed it down the drain. I had short hair: since then, I've kept it long enough to cover my ears...!

Another night, I woke up and something was picking its way through my hair. That time, it was a big pine beetle. I flicked him off and sent him sailing across the room!

Keeping spiders, etc., out is a good reason to have the woodpile away from the house. On the other hand, you don't want it so far away that you can't easily get to it in bad weather. If you don't have a woodshed, at least set yourself up so you can tarp the stuff.

It's also nice to get come pallets to stack it on, to keep it up out of the mud. Wood needs to dry out, or "season" to burn properly. We've found that wood that's so old there's no bark left on it is ideal when the stove is cold and you need it to get hot fast. After that, you want to load it with regular, dry firewood, that won't burn quite as hot, but will burn longer. If you find yourself stuck with wood that's gotten rained on or is still green, mix it with the driest wood you've got, after the dry wood is burning well.

Then there are the ashes. My stove has to be cleaned out every other day when I'm using it daily/nightly. I'm lucky; my stove has a drawer under the firebox. I pull that out, empty it into a bucket and take it outside. My neighbor has to clean out the firebox with his fire going. It's messy, hot, and dangerous; it's easy to knock coals out onto the floor.

You need a metal bucket for the ashes and coals, and you want to set it away from anything flammable. One year, somebody nearby lost their beautiful log cabin, because they set their ash bucket on the porch and then went off to work. The porch was wood; there were, not surprisingly, hot coals in the bucket, and there it all went.

I toss a handful of creosote eater into the stove at intervals recommended on the container, or sooner, if I see the stuff building up: it's greasy-looking. We had one chimney fire, and let me tell you; that's exactly one more than you want to deal with, so use that creosote eater, even if you think your wood is burning clean!

Get yourself one of those wire brushes for cleaning out the stove pipe: they come in 6-inch or 8-inch diameters, depending on the size of the pipe. You can do this any time, but for sure, do it either in the spring, after you're through with the stove for the season, or in the fall, before you need it again. I recommend doing it in the spring. That way, if there's a cold snap earlier than you expected, you're all set and don't have to drop something else to take care of the stove pipe before you can fire up the stove.

My stove has a glass door, that lets you see the fire (sort of; it's "frosted" glass). That sounded so romantic at one time. Now, it's just a way to see how the fire is getting along, without having to open the door and look. Other than that, I pretty much spend the winter trying not to think about the days when I could walk over to the wall and adjust a thermostat....

CHAPTER 6: Water

Here in northern Arizona, we haul water. It isn't that you can't drill a well, but drilling is ruinously expensive. There's a lot of volcanic rock, and the aquifers are way down deep. To haul, you need a tank intended for the purpose, and a vehicle stout enough to carry it. This can be a trailer or a truck. For us, the best thing has been to have a dedicated water trailer, which we pull with our old one ton truck. That's the thing about using a trailer: you need a towing vehicle that's up to the job. If you think your little 4-cylinder "crossover" can pull a heavy load, you may be right. The key isn't pulling, however, it's <u>stopping</u>. Get a heavy load, like water, rolling, and you'd better have something in front of it that can dig in its heels and stop that thang.

My friend is a retired mechanic, so he's able to keep both truck and trailer going. We lost count a long time ago of all the broken springs and associated suspension parts, the number of brake pads and the flat (shredded) tires. Our hauling tank holds 1200 gallons and water weighs almost 9 pounds a gallon, so it doesn't take a lot of math skill to see the problem. We try our best not to have to haul with any water remaining inside the hauling tank. That's because water, in addition to being heavy, doesn't sit still and behave if it has room to move around in the tank. If you have a few hundred gallons in the tank and go around a corner faster than you may have intended, controlling your rig can become exciting! I myself don't drive this rig. I have argued for years for a spare, alternative, smaller rig, say; a 300 or 500-gallon tank. That's plenty heavy enough for someone who isn't used to handling a truck and trailer, much less a cargo that takes some finessing My friend is sure he will always be young enough, fit enough, and able-bodied enough to drive the rig he has. (I know; right)?

We have a 1500-gallon holding tank. The hauling tank is used to fill this house tank and for water for the animal pens. We park the trailer at a high enough point that it can gravity feed the water line to the pens. If that weren't possible, we'd need a pump, and the power to run it, in order to move water from the hauling tank through the water lines.

Each horse's lean-to also has a rainwater catchment arrangement attached to its roof. These fill smaller (100 to 300 gallon tanks). In a pinch, we can water the horses with this water, and from time to time we've had to, but normally, this roof runoff is reserved for gardening and the greenhouse. We've only needed to use hauled water during two of the last ten years in order to water our plants, so I strongly recommend that you set up some of these rain barrels/tanks. One caveat here: in some locales, harvesting rainwater is considered the equivalent of "diverting a stream," and is illegal! Check those regs.

Hauling water will change your attitude, if you're accustomed to taking water for granted. For example, we sponge bathe during the week, and reserve a shower or tub bath, including hair washing, for once a week. You take a shower by running the water enough to get wet; then turning it off, soaping up, and turning the water back on to rinse. We use low-flow toilets, of course. Our original plan was to use composting toilets, but we were told the county doesn't allow them. We found out too late that yes, it does: had we approached the Health Department and gotten a permit, we could have had composting toilets. Silly us; we went to the Building Department. If you know anybody that has a set up like the one you want, by all means, pick their brains about the technicalities.

So; if you can't afford a well, and you live in a water haul area, you'll need a hauling tank and a holding tank. How much you pay for these will depend on a number of factors, so you'll need to do some research. Which company you buy from, what size and shape of tank, as well as whether you can pick up the tank or have to have it shipped will all affect the price. You'll need a water trailer and a truck to pull it with. You could also set your hauling tank on a flatbed truck, which you would then only use to haul water. Some people do this, but we have always used a water trailer, and kept our truck free for other work around the place.

We do get one nice break in Arizona; you're not required to buy tags for your water trailer. I guess they figure if you couldn't afford the tags, you'd go without water, and that would be wrong. It isn't like bureaucrats to care about such things, so take that as subject to change, and check to make sure that law hasn't been amended or repealed before you assume you don't need that tag, if you live in Arizona. Elsewhere, find out what the laws are like there.

If you're hauling, you also need to find out where the standpipes are, and how they work. There are two in the little town nearest us. One is coin operated, and has a pipe for filling the hauling tank on your vehicle, and a small vending area for filling gallon and five-gallon jugs for your house or camp. The other standpipe location has a card reader. You sign up and pay a fee, and they give you a card to use when you fill up your tank. Once a month, they send you a bill for what you've taken. At least here, you end up getting water for your money. In another town not far away, you pay a fat fee for the card, and all that gets you is the card; water is extra.

Delivery

Our other option would be to have water delivered to us. There are several companies that provide this service. One guy we talked to about five years ago said it cost him $100 to have water hauled to his place. We weren't clear if that included the water, but we suspected it didn't. Water is pretty reasonable here. The costs of fuel and vehicle repairs and maintenance are not, however, so it's fair to assume that a good share, if not all, of that hundred bucks goes to keep the hauler in business. In a pinch, of course, we would pay: we and our animals need water, so whatever it cost, we'd have to go for it. (I hope my friend is right about his super powers and eternal youth...).

Some people drink the water as it comes out the tap, directly from their hauling tank. Our hauling tank is black, which helps inhibit the growth of algae, but there's still some algae in it. We run the water into our house tank and then into the line for the house, with an inline filter to keep the algae and sediment out, but we still don't risk drinking it from the tap. Water for drinking or cooking comes through its own small tap, via another filter under the sink. We've had to replace our water pump once in ten years, and our under-sink filter every six months. Our water is really hard; even after being filtered, it scales up the coffee pot and the tea kettle pretty quickly. About once a week, we have to let them stand with a vinegar solution that breaks down the minerals so we can clean them up. It's not hard to do; it's just one more thing.

When we lived on the smaller place we had before this one, we had water hauled, because it was cheaper (we were much closer to a paved road, for one thing). If you have to have water delivered, know your usage, so you will know when to order. You're also going to have to develop a "weather eye." If a storm is coming, even though you may not be clear out of water, you may want to have the guy top up your tank, in case bad roads keep him from reaching you for awhile.

Our water hauler had plenty of stories about people who would discover only <u>after</u> a heavy rain that they were out of water and insist that he bring them a load immediately. When he would politely inform them that their crappy road was one big bog and he wasn't willing to risk getting stuck and not being able to service his other customers, it pissed them off. Well; too bad for them. The ones that fired him and hired another hauler soon found out their new guy wasn't any more willing to risk it than he was, just because they refused to get a clue. If there's a storm coming, and you aren't sure you have enough water to get you through a period when the hauler can't get to you (or when you can't get in and out with your own rig), it's time to get water! There's no excuse for running out, especially if animals and other people are depending on you to take care of things, so get a clue.

If you are lucky enough to be able to drill a well, or to find yourself with a piece of property that has a well, you'll need to get it tested from time to time. The wells in Arizona, at least in these parts, often have a certain amount of arsenic. You have to get your wells tested to make sure the concentration is safe. The county and state also probably have testing requirements of their own, so make sure you find out what they are, and abide by them, because they'll condemn your well if there's anything about it they don't like.

Having a well doesn't necessarily mean you'll have running water at usable pressure. We had friends in central Arizona whose well only came in at a trickle. They had to have a cistern, or holding tank, so the trickle could fill it up to where they could pump that water into the house. They had to be every bit as careful as we do to monitor their water usage. Get ahead of the ability of that trickle to fill the cistern, and you can wait, wait, and wait some more, for the tank to fill back up.

There's no way around it; there's only a finite amount of water available on this old planet. We're all – city and country folk alike - going to wake up sooner or later to that fact, and we'll have to stop using water to flush away our waste, grow grass so our neighbors will envy our yards, and to wash our cars. We're going to have to ditch the idea that it's okay to frack for oil, which not only wastes water, but contaminates aquifers. We're going to have to *get* the idea that we're all responsible for using water wisely, or we're all going to run out of water. If you're living off grid, you'll be at the front of this particular learning curve, so that's all to the good.

CHAPTER 7: Animals

<u>Other People's Animals</u>

I don't know how many places still have Open Range laws, but Arizona does. That means cattlemen are free to let their animals roam, and if you don't want them on your land, it's up to you to fence them out. Why might you object to cows straying onto your land? Well, the problems we've run into include cows trampling and eating our plants, and breaking into our hay storage and helping themselves. Chasing them off is a no-no, under Arizona Revised Statutes 3-1311. Any person that sees your <u>dog</u> chasing a bovine can legally shoot your dog!

Being on a low fixed income as we are, we budget our money to the penny. It's hard to describe the sickening feeling of seeing some dumb cow-brute scattering/pooping on and eating the finite supply of hay that you bought for your horses. Hay that you can only replace by dipping into your own grocery money – our only budget variable.

It didn't help, when we were living at the old place, when a local cattle grower's horse strayed onto our land one day. Of course, we didn't know whose horse this was, only that he was lost. We dished out some of our precious hay and water to him, and started trying to find the owner. We called the livestock officer, and put up flyers. After several days, the cattleman's wife very haughtily deigned to come get the horse. We got not so much as a thank you. We didn't expect, and wouldn't have accepted, money for caring for the horse. We would have <u>hoped</u>, had our situations been reversed, to have our own animal cared for as attentively (like that would have happened with this nasty woman), but, damn; not to even say anything....

An acquaintance who lived in the same area found one of these people's steers with his hoof caught in a cattle guard. Fearing that the animal would panic and break his leg if left alone, the guy stayed on the scene and spent several hours working to get the steer free. Once that was done, he alerted the rancher that this animal might need further attention for cuts and bruises from the misadventure. Again; not so much as a "thank you."

It doesn't take many encounters like this to make you feel like cattle ranchers are the scourge of the earth. Thankfully, we have only run in to this one couple of idiots, so I can attest that most are much nicer folks than them. When we first moved out here to the Forty, a friend who had come to visit called on his way home to report having seen a cow "with her insides hanging out." It was calving time, and we were pretty sure what he'd seen was a cow that had just had a calf, and was passing the afterbirth. As soon as we could, we put out feelers as to who was running cattle out here and how we could contact him in an emergency. The guy appreciated our interest, and we had only the most civil interactions with him, and since, with his successor.

There's still that Open Range law, though, that can put you on the wrong side of the law if you have an untoward encounter with livestock, so follow the old adage, 'cause it's right on the money: "Good fences make good neighbors." Build a fence.

If you move out into the country, city people can still cause you grief. For whatever reason, some city folks think if they're tired of their dog/cat/whatever, the thing to do isn't to take them to the pound or a rescue, or find them a new home, but to dump them – on your doorstep. Some of our nicest dogs have come to us after being dumped by assholes that think, "out of sight, out of mind." In fact, we got the two goats we have now when they wandered into the yard one day. We're miles from the nearest maintained road. We'll never know if these guys made it all the way here on their own (in an area lousy with coyotes, not to mention larger predators), or if some asshole hauled them right to our gate before dropping them off.

Either way, animal abandoners are going to be a fact of your life if you live in the country. If you can't keep or don't want these animals, please care for them until you can get them to a shelter or to animal control so they have a chance of finding a home.

<u>Your Animals</u>

Just because your nearest neighbor lives out of sight down the road, doesn't mean you aren't obliged to control/monitor your dog. We have always penned or, temporarily, chained up, our dogs, and we've always had stupid neighbors who flout the leash laws and let their dogs run loose. One neighbor's dog killed some of our chickens and two of our barn cats.

And, we almost lost a dog because of someone else's refusal to control their dog. One day, my husband was looking out the window. He got up with an odd look on his face, and told me, "There's a guy with a gun in our yard."

We went outside and sure enough, there was a grim-looking man out there, staring at Christopher, one of our dogs, who was in his pen. My husband asked if he could help the guy, and the fellow told us a black and tan dog had just killed his wife's cat right in front of her. (Christopher was black and tan). My husband said, "Well, as you can see, our dogs are penned up, and also; they're cat-friendly." (Thank goodness, two of our barn cats were in Christopher's pen, one of them cuddled right up to him). The guy took all this in and agreed that <u>our</u> black and tan dog apparently wasn't the one he was after.

God knows if he'd have come to this conclusion if he'd come skulking around when we weren't there to point out the obvious to him.... All because of some jerk that let his dog run loose.

Some people assume that if you live outside of town there are no leash laws. Others think, just because the dog catcher isn't liable to come rolling by, they can ignore the leash law. Either way, in the city as in the country, bad neighbors can make life hell for everybody else.

Predators are another problem. There are raptors (hawks and eagles) that are big enough to kill a small dog or a cat. If you allow your pets outside, make sure they have a fenced yard, and keep an eye on them. A moment's inattention here is no safer than it is when you're tending a young child. In fact, as a friend of mine once said, "a dog is a fuzzy two-year-old!" No matter how scary-smart your two-year-old may be, they don't know there are BAD THINGS in the world that will get them. You know about the BAD THINGS, and it's up to you to watch over them.

For a dog or cat living in the city, the bad things include traffic, evil people, and hazardous locations that can trap them. For the same animals living in the country, the dangers can include all those things and more. Don't assume just because the "traffic" consists of one or two cars a month instead of dozens per hour that the odds favor a creature that knows nothing about mass and momentum, not to mention driver inattention. In addition to those hazards, there are the raptors mentioned above, along with coyotes, and poisonous snakes. Depending on where you live, you can add mountain lions, bears, gators and more to that list. Then, as I mentioned above, if your dog chases a bovine and some cowboy sees it, your dog can get shot, perfectly legally. Please be a responsible petparent.

Speaking of cats; sad to say that some people believe that if you feed a cat, s/he won't hunt. By nature, some cats are hunters and some are not. If your cat is a hunter, you won't be able to deter him, no matter how fat and lazy you think he is: let him outside, and he'll prove it. If your cat is not a hunter, denying him food is stupid and cruel, and won't change his nature. It's pretty easy to keep more than one cat, and doing so will increase your chances of having at least one mouser. And if nothing else, as noted below, you'll still be better off because you have pets. Take care of them, and they take care of you.

NOTE: Some think that pet ownership is, and should be, a privilege of the rich. In some communities, if you have a pet, they will deny you food stamps. Food stamps can't be used to buy pet food. They're scared to death you will use some of the little money you have for your furbaby. (Those people think spending your own money as you wish is also a privilege to be reserved for the rich). In fact, numerous studies have demonstrated that having a pet confers real, measurable health benefits. If you have a pet, you are more likely to survive a heart attack, for one example. It's just another way for this country to show its contempt for the poor, and for innocent animals. Don't apologize to anybody for having, and loving, animals.

Equines

I've mentioned the need to supervise and protect your smaller pets. What about the big ones?

If your dream of country life, like ours, includes horses, welcome to the club. If we lived in the city, we wouldn't be able to have even one horse. We spend a monthly amount per horse that is a third or less than it would cost to pay to board them in the city. We have more than one horse, which is good because they're herd animals, and not happy alone. If you can't afford and don't want more than one horse, you can provide a goat for company, as most horses like goats. Donkeys, or, as we in the Southwest call them, burros, would also be good companions for your horse (and for you), but their needs are very different.

Healthy burros need only grass hay. If fed grain, they can develop unsightly and disfiguring fatty lumps that don't go away. In addition, burros can't tolerate some meds that will work for horses,

50

and you will need a vet that understands this. Burros dislike dogs, equating them with coyotes, so keep your dogs away from them: burros kill coyotes. Burros do like people, and make wonderful pets in their own right. If I'd discovered burros long before I did, I'd have them now instead of horses. A woman who often travels to South America told me a shaman she met there calls the burro the philosopher of the animal kingdom. From my experience, this makes sense. If you haven't checked out the burro, see the Resources section at the end of this book for a couple of places where you can find out more about, and perhaps adopt, one of these very special animals.

Fences and Pens, Etc.:

Here are some things to keep in mind as far as accommodations for your large animals. First, you need secure fences. We went with electric fences because they were the cheapest we could find, both to install and to maintain. You can do as we did, and get a solar fence charger pretty reasonably. Ours handles four big pens and also the perimeter of our property. We went with a braided, rope-type material rather than wire, because it's easier for us and the animals to see, although it does cost a bit more. We used T-posts, although our veterinarian disapproved. T-posts are relatively cheap, and we had no trouble finding protective caps and insulators for them. No; these aren't the safest posts for animals; a horse can rear up, either in play or reacting to something frightening, come down and impale him/herself on one of these posts. Wooden posts are safer, but will eventually rot and have to be replaced. Large-diameter pipe would be somewhat safer than T-posts, but also more expensive. They make insulators for these better posts as well: we were very limited in our budget for fencing, and we took the calculated risk of using T-posts. To date, there haven't been any problems, but if you can get your hands on better, safer, posts, do it.

From time to time, you will need to check to see that your

fence is charging, and the devices for doing this are quite reasonably priced. If the fence isn't charging, you will need to walk or ride your fence line to find out what the problem is. During a wet spell, weeds and grass that are soaked can short out the fence. We have also had large wildlife come through and, probably in a panic, pull an insulator away from a tree and drop the line into the mud. The nice thing is; these fences are pretty easy to repair and maintain, as I said.

If electric fencing doesn't appeal to you, and you prefer wood pole or rail fences, I still recommend running a "hot" wire along the top. Horses will rub a fence to scratch themselves, or lean into it trying to reach grass on the other side, or they will bump into it, lunging at a rival on the other side. It doesn't take much of this to weaken even a pretty stout fence, and an electric wire running along the top will discourage this kind of wear and tear, saving your horses from injury and you from a lot of work and expense!

Wire fences are my least favorite for horses. Wire stretches and sags. It can become so loose that a horse may try to walk over or through it, and become entangled and injured. Wire can fatigue and break, and cause puncture wounds that can easily become infected, or tear skin and muscle, requiring expensive vet visits and lengthy after-care from you. Field fencing, a common kind of pasture fencing, is fairly cheap for a hundred-foot roll, so you may be tempted to go with that. If you have any alternative, though, please don't go with wire fencing for horses. If that's the way you have to go, then I hope you'll run a hot wire along the top.

Barb-wire is horrible; I don't care if somebody offers you the stuff for free, tell them no thanks. By the way; if you're out riding in cattle country, watch out for it: there are people, who, if they just have part of a roll left, will leave it on the ground, rather than pack it home with them. It's one of the nastier things to encounter when you're out riding, especially if grass or weeds conceal it until your horse steps into it. Best to stay on the trails!

How big a pen to build? That depends somewhat on the

amount of fencing material you have available, but go as big as you can. Horses in the wild travel for miles a day, in search of water and grass. Then humans domesticate them, put them in a twelve-by-twelve – or smaller! - box stall and pat themselves on the back for giving the horse so much "room!" Our pens are 100 feet wide and 40 feet long. We turn the horses and mule out to roam the Forty most mornings after feeding, but when that isn't possible for whatever reason, there's room in their pens for them to run and play.

A barn isn't really needed unless you live in the far north. A lean-to, with one side closed to the prevailing winds and a roof for shade, is perfectly adequate. It snows here, and our horses sometimes stand out in the weather, and sometimes opt to get under their lean-tos and avoid it. We figure they know what they want and need, and it's up to them.

We don't blanket our horses. If you choose to blanket your horse from time to time, it should go without saying that you never leave a blanketed horse unsupervised. A blanketed horse can be injured (for instance, trying to scratch his belly and trapping his hoof in the blanket and panicking). He/she can also become overheated, and need to have that blanket removed. In our experience, unless a horse is actually sick, there is no need to blanket them, and in that case, of course, we're going to be supervising the heck out of them. Those who show their horses and blanket them to keep them clean, are not our kind of people, so their values don't concern us. I'm going to assume that if you're poor, your horse is poor(!) and you're not a horse show diva, so you aren't worried about having spotless animals 24/7.

In my experience and observation, there's no furbaby so big that a petparent can avoid the responsibility of baby-proofing!

By the way: DO NOT advertise an equine "free to good home." Although it's illegal to slaughter horses in most of the US at this writing, plenty of money grubbers are trying to reinstate the practice. If you're near the Mexican border, equines are vulnerable to being trucked across and butchered.   There's a dismayingly large number of rescues for all kinds and sizes of animals, so more likely than not, the effort to place them somewhere safe will pay off, and literally be a lifesaver.

Milk Cows and Goats

Some of you may remember the flap years ago about dosing dairy cows with hormones to make them give more milk. When the veterinary association gave the practice their stamp of approval, I was dismayed and flaggergasted. In case you don't know your cows, those big black and white ladies you see in commercials for dairy products are Holsteins. Other breeds include the Ayrshire, the Guernsey, and the Jersey. Commercial dairies almost all use Holsteins. Why? They're the biggest ones, and the ones that give the most milk. A Holstein cow *without benefit of additional hormonal enhancement* will give up to four gallons of milk a day, more than any other breed. Of course, for the "agri-business" crowd, there's never "enough".

So, okay; you want your own milker. Unless you have a large household, you won't want a cow. I was friends years ago with a couple that wanted their own dairy products. Well, she did: she wanted the milk, plus she wanted to make her own butter and farmer's cheese, and so her husband bought her not one, but two cows! Not only didn't he get her a nice little Jersey, he got her two Holsteins! For days, they were calling everybody they knew and begging us to "come get some milk! Come get some butter! Please!"

It wasn't long before one of the two cows was sold. The woman still had trouble processing all that milk, and not long after that, she gave up on the idea of having a milker, and the second cow was gone as well.

I don't know why they didn't think of a smaller cow, like the Jersey, or a milk goat, or goats. Perhaps they'd heard that goat's milk doesn't taste good. Actually, it does. We had a milk goat, and her milk was just as sweet and wholesome as any cow's milk. The key is twofold; feed her the same high-quality hay and grain you would feed a milk cow (only far less of it), and, as with a milk cow, gently wash her udder before milking her. That's all: control her diet, and keep her clean. It ain't rocket science.

A milker, whether a cow or a goat, needs to be milked twice a day to avoid drying up or developing mastitis. Also; she will eventually dry up in any case, necessitating finding her a baby daddy: when she has that new baby, she has milk for that baby. Of course then, you get to figure out what to do with Baby. Her first milk after giving birth should go to her young; it includes immune factors that the little one needs to survive and thrive, which is important, even if Baby's eventual destiny is the freezer. It's a lot better to keep a meat animal healthy than to dose them up with antibiotics and hormones, which is why a lot of us have backed away from the meat produced by Big Ag.

This need to deal with the baby was what finally prompted me to give up on the idea of having a milk goat, much as I enjoyed the milk. Then too, we had to be there twice a day at the same times for milking. We never had a very active social life, but every absence from the property had to be planned around the milking schedule.

Unless someone is available and willing to stay home and tend to such chores, it's hard to have large animals. It's well worth it, if that's what you enjoy, but be sure you know what you're getting into. And, for heaven's sake, either don't get such animals if you're not sure, or, if you get them and then decide it's not going to work, take care of them while you find new homes for them, or shelters/rescues that can take them.

Miscellany

Transporting Livestock: If you have horses, cows, or other livestock, you will find that they need to be hauled/transported from time to time, for instance, to the vet. (If the vet comes out, expect to pay a trip charge, in addition to whatever s/he charges for services rendered). If you are experienced in hauling livestock yourself, you may want to invest in a horse trailer or a stock trailer. If not, hire it done.

There are several reasons for this. For one thing, hauling livestock isn't like hauling your stuff on moving day. Animals may not stand quietly in the trailer, and a driver must be able to handle the rig safely when they shift their weight. The driver also needs to consider that, in order to keep their footing in the trailer, animals need time to react when the rig turns, changes lanes, stops, etc.

Trailers need to be inspected often for safety. Old, worn hitches must be replaced. Floors need to be cleaned with each use, because animal waste can help rot trailer floors. It isn't unknown for a trailer floor to give out under a horse (see various horse magazines for some of these horror stories; I don't have the stomach to repeat them here). If you lack hauling experience, and/or the means to keep your trailer absolutely ship shape, you will want to hire someone reputable to haul your animals.

Wormers, etc.: Horses need meds from time to time, and need to be wormed once in awhile. Between my friend and me, we have decades of experience with horses, and even so, we almost maimed one of our dogs through our ignorance about horse wormers. I'm talking about those measured-dose tubes you can buy at any feed store. We wormed our horses awhile back. We didn't think anything of administering the doses to our horses; as I said, it's part of a horse person's routine. A couple of our horses, when we squirted the paste into the corner of their mouths, slung their heads, and little globs of the stuff went flying. Within the hour, my friend called to my attention that one of our dog's pupils were completely dilated.

We called the vet and when they found out we'd wormed the horses, they said bring her in NOW. Apparently, she'd licked up one of the globs of the goo, and it poisoned her. Our vet couldn't guarantee that her eyesight would come back (Thankfully, it did).

When we expressed surprise that the stuff was so dangerous, he said that he knew many horse people who had killed their dogs with horse wormer. They see on the label that it contains ivermectin, which is in the heart worm medicine dogs get, and they say, "Heck; I'll just save some money and give the dog a lick of this stuff while I'm at it."

Trouble is; the drug is WAY more concentrated in the horse wormer than it is in heart worm medicine for dogs.... The one we used smelled like green apples. I had better sense, but it still crossed mymind to wonder if it tasted as good as it smelled. Imagine a young child getting hold of the stuff. Personally, I think it has no business being sold over the counter, and that it should be administered only by a vet.

Again; we aren't novices. We've wormed horses for years and never, ever, heard that this could be dangerous. So; dear friends, if you give your horses paste wormers, leave the dogs and little kids in the house, and if any winds up anywhere but in your horse's mouth, clean it up!

CHAPTER 8: Gardens and Greenhouses and Food Generally

Eating well when you're poor is a challenge. If, like us, you've ever had to go the food bank route, you know what I mean. Too many times what they send you home with could be accompanied by a cookbook called, "101 Ways to Ingest Sugar and Starch." Only one food bank we went to ever asked us to fill out a questionnaire. They made sure we got very <u>little</u> sugar and starch (my ex was diabetic), and lots of canned and fresh veggies. For families with babies and toddlers, they included fresh and powdered milk. They also furnished dog and cat food for petparents. Sadly; for administrative reasons, this food bank eventually closed. Most of the ones that are in business send people home with plenty of bread, cookies, candy, pasta, snack cakes, etc. It makes me crazy when people rag on poor folks for being fat. I'd like to see anybody manage to stay fit and trim when they're obliged to get their calories from sugar and starch. For too many people, these cheaply priced products make the difference between going hungry and having something on the table from payday to payday. At least, if you live in the country, you can provide yourself with some real food.

<u>Gardens</u>

In-ground gardening is labor – and water – intensive, so I'm not a fan. Even now that I'm retired, I won't do it: it just doesn't make sense to me. Raised beds and container gardens are much easier to deal with, take less water, and still produce enough food, herbs, and flowers to be worth the effort.

Raised beds that are underlined with plastic will retain water longer around the roots of your plants, saving both water and money. Arranging the beds and containers with space between for walking or wheeling a little cart can save you time and make things a lot easier on your back. You can start the big stuff, like pumpkins and melons, in the greenhouse or cold frames and then transfer them to raised beds.

Things like corn, you'll probably want to start outside. In that case (as well as for your raised beds), you'll need a varmint-proof fence.

Years ago, I went to a farm to pick up a load of hay. As the men were loading it, I remarked to the farmer, "You've got songbirds!" I was surprised, because, sadly, fewer and fewer places can one go to and hear birdsong. The man said, "Look at the corners of my fields." I did; in the corners, he or his employees had steered well out from the fences, leaving pockets of grain in these areas. He told me, "I can't tell you how many of my neighbors have remarked on the fact that I have songbirds, but they don't. Yet, they'll harvest every last leaf and blade, and every grain, right up into the tightest corners. Bird's just like you and me: in order to live someplace, he's got to have something to eat!" I've never forgotten that, and I hope you won't, either. Please consider sowing/planting a few things outside your garden fence that the wild things can have.

Greenhouses

Our greenhouse keeps us in tomatoes, peppers, leaf lettuce, and Swiss chard between paydays. It's nice, because living in a food desert (more than 35 miles from the nearest supermarket), and being on a fixed income, we typically buy groceries once a month. Before we had our greenhouse, we ran out of fresh produce about a week and a half after payday. Just as important to us as access to fresh produce, is our ability to control the kind of produce we eat. By growing as much of our own food as possible, we are able to keep from consuming the genetically-modified "frankenfoods" that are foisted off on the public by Big Agriculture. We buy heirloom seeds, and we save seeds. If that doesn't seem like a big deal, consider: if we were commercial farmers, we could actually be sued for doing this!

Our greenhouse is hydroponic. We used to think hydroponics was for rich people, being horribly expensive to set up. Then we attended a seminar at a local hydroponics store (see Resources, below), and found out there are options for people like us. It would be nice to have all the timers and automatic feeders, etc., but it's possible to get along without them, and we do. By using a substrate of coco fiber and perlite to hold moisture and physically support the roots, we are able to feed/water our plants by the cupful, instead of using a hose or even a watering can. If you've never looked into this kind of plant maintenance, check it out. It's proven to be a blessing to us, saving gallons of precious water, and taking only minutes of attention a day.

Even if you aren't set up for hydroponic gardening, using a greenhouse can make your life a lot easier. Having your plants indoors under conditions as controlled as you can manage (again; lighting, etc., can be a challenge if you're off grid), makes the most of your resources. Years ago I heard about a man in one of the northern states that had a big greenhouse and raised rabbits. He gave the rabbits the run of the place, rather than confining them in cages or hutches: they can't climb, so were no threat to his plants. He added their droppings to his potting soils, and their body heat protected the plants from the cold in the winter. (Presumably, he had to do something to provide good ventilation/air flow in the summer, to keep the rabbits from having heatstroke. Then again; he raised them for meat, so maybe there just weren't that many rabbits in the warmer months...).

Animal Feed: Fodder

So far, we haven't been able to make it work, but you can supplement your animals' (horses, goats, pigs, chickens) with barley grass fodder. The problems we've run into include mold, and low yields. The commercial set-ups are costly enough to be out of reach of people like us, but we're still working on it. A bag of barley is a lot easier to handle and cheaper than bales of hay, and will produce a lot of fodder. It wouldn't replace hay entirely, but would save us a ton of money, and in the winter, would provide our animals with green, living food that would otherwise not be available. Check into this if you have animals and see if you can come up with a way to make it work for you.

Preserving Your Food

When we moved to our first off grid place, in our motor home, we had the propane refrigerator that was in it. We're still using it. It's the size of a large dorm fridge, so we're really limited in space. We haven't upgraded because a full-size propane fridge is beyond our means to buy, and the solar-powered refrigerator I want also costs more than we can afford, and would require more panels, and probably at least one dedicated battery (since our existing array is insufficient to provide power 24/7). Although I'm sure the modern propane refrigerators are very efficient, it would still mean paying for more propane. I refuse to do that, when, you know; sunshine costs NOTHING per "gallon!"

My grandmother and three of her daughters were prize-winning canners, taking home ribbons for their food from the county fair every year. My mother, however, never learned to can. She had her sights set on a life as anything but a farmer's wife, and refused to learn this humble skill. If she had learned to can, I probably would have learned as well. Thank heaven, she didn't! Canning is about the worst way to preserve food there is.

Canned food has to be heated to such a high temperature that most of the nutrients are destroyed. And, even if canned food looks and tastes absolutely scrumptious, it can kill you. My Grandma and my aunts knew what they were doing, but not everyone who cans is as good as them (and yes; I know people have been home canning food and eating it with no problems for generations). I just don't think it's a good way to preserve food.

Freezing is pretty good, if you can afford the propane or have enough solar panels to run a freezer. Freezing retains many more nutrients than does canning. All you have to do is make sure your packaging is air tight to prevent freezer burn. You can also protect your food from freezer burn by putting the date on each package, and making sure you use up the oldest first. Also, of course, there can't be any interruption of power. If power is lost, stay out of the freezer! Keep it buttoned up until power is restored; then open it and check. If it was off long enough for stuff to defrost, you're going to want to have a BIG cookout.

Dehydration works well, too; dehydrated food retains most of its nutrients. You can find plans to build solar dehydrators, so as not to expend any fuel or electricity to do the job. You need air-tight and water-tight containers to store your dried food, and you should dust it with food-grade diatomaceous earth before sealing it up. Diatomaceous earth kills any weevils, etc., that may hatch in your food, and all you have to do is rinse it off before cooking. If a little diatomaceous earth remains, it's harmless to us humans.

Water Glass

Not many people know it nowadays, but you can preserve extra eggs in "water glass," which is a solution of liquid sodium silicate. We've never had enough eggs to have a surplus, because we've only had from two to four hens laying at any one time, and with only two people, they simply never got that far ahead of us. (In the winter, when they don't lay that many eggs, due to the cold and long nights, we simply purchase extra cage free eggs).

From what I've read, you can't preserve store-bought eggs this way, because they've been cleaned so throroughly. Eggs come from the hen with a natural coating that preserves them, and commercial egg producers wash this off. When you get eggs from your hens, don't wash them! If the eggs are soiled, simply wipe them briskly with a piece of flannel or other rag, and put them in the fridge. They will keep pretty well compared with store-bought eggs, as long as you don't remove this coating until you're ready to use them. For people who can't keep up with their hens' egg production, water glass may just be the answer to keeping extra eggs to tide you over through the winter when your hens are waiting for spring to come again!

By the way; if you don't have electricity 24/7, don't try raising those cute little chicks the feed stores sell every spring. Without warmth, they won't survive. As an alternative, buy some young hens from someone you can trust (so you don't get stuck with their old hens that have stopped laying). As you need additional chickens, you'll need a rooster. Then, let certain of your hens "brood," over their eggs until they hatch, and let them raise their babies. Make sure everyone who collects eggs knows which eggs are being left to hatch, to prevent the gruesome mistake of breaking the wrong ones into the skillet...!

There are lots of resources now for people who want to raise their own chickens and eggs, so do your homework.

Fermentation/culturing

I used to make yogurt. In June of 2013, I discovered milk kefir, and that was the end of home made yogurt for me. Yogurt requires a lot more work and has to culture in a heated environment, like in an oven with a pilot light, or in an electric yogurt maker. Milk kefir cultures at room temperature, and has many times more beneficial organisms than yogurt. (That's not true of the kefir you see in the dairy case; it's a mix of yogurt and kefir, and has far fewer beneficial organisms than the home made stuff). You can also make a tasty "cream cheese" by straining your kefir through a coffee filter. There are places on the Internet that will tell you how. You can reserve the whey from doing this to use as a starter in making your fermented veggies, if you don't do "wild" fermentations, as I prefer to do.

If you have extra milk, you can make "farmers cheese," which is very similar to ricotta, and again, you can find websites and videos on the 'Net that will tell you how. (The whey from this, however, won't do for fermenting veggies: it doesn't have the micro organisms in it that kefir whey has). The sites I visited said you could make farmers cheese using either white vinegar or lemon juice. I don't bother with lemon juice: when the cheese is done, there's no flavor remaining to indicate whether vinegar or lemon juice was used, so why waste the lemons?

After a few months of eating kefir and other fermented/cultured foods, I had far less misery when nasal allergy season rolled around. I was all excited to tell my doctor, but she was like, totally unimpressed. Her assistant, however, agreed with me that it's crucial to have a healthy gut if you want to be healthy over all. I have since read of other people who started eating fermented foods and had the same experience I did, in terms of allergy relief. Will it work as well for you? Who knows: the only thing we have in common is, we're all different, but there's more evidence all the time that you can't be healthy without good gut flora.

When I started out, I made a sauerkraut-like mix of red and green cabbage with carrots, all finely shredded. It was tasty, but I kept trying new recipes. Now I make Hot Garden Mix; florets of broccoli and cauliflower, with chunks of carrots and jalapeños, with crushed red pepper for a little extra kick. I also make brined garlic dill pickles, and kimchi, among others.

Beyond the possible health benefits, fermented foods are user-friendly. If they look good, smell good, and taste good, they're good. If they turn out slimy, or develop black mold, it wouldn't be a good idea to eat them, but you wouldn't want to do that anyway. I've had three or four batches fail, and I hate to lose out on having the food, but I don't cry about it. Far more of my fermentations have turned out great. I just compost the bad ones and start over. Get a good book, like <u>Wild Fermentation</u>, by Sandor Katz. His book got me started, and it's still my Bible, when it comes to fermentation. It's easy, it's fun, and you end up with good healthy food throughout the month, so you don't have to worry if payday is a ways off and you don't have enough fresh stuff till then.

On several of the forums I've visited, moms are amazed to note that their finicky kids – and husbands – <u>love</u> eating fermented/cultured veggies! By the way; I understand that fermented foods are considered raw, so if you're a raw foodie, don't let that keep you from checking out this great way of preserving, and enhancing, your food.

A Note About Animals as Food

We don't raise animals for food (if you don't count the eggs from our chickens). This is partly because we don't eat that much meat, and because commercially produced meat is full of hormones, drugs, etc., that we don't want to ingest.

We have talked about hunting: lots of difference between killing a wild animal and killing one that has been able to trust you all its life! Unfortunately, the licenses are expensive, not to mention we might not even get a tag. Then, after you've field dressed your kill (you have to remove the guts to help keep it from spoiling before it's finished), there's also the hassle of getting your kill back to the vehicle. An elk can dress out at over 700 pounds, so you're not going to throw him/her over your shoulder! Finally, there's the matter of finding and paying a meat cutter who knows how to process game so it ends up fit to eat.

If you want to raise meat animals and/or hunt, you'll have to do your own homework. 'Scuse me while I go check on the beans....

CHAPTER 9: Security

<u>The Less Said, The Better</u>

If you're like most people, you're fairly guileless. That's either because you were brought up to be polite and sociable, or because you're not a predator, or both. We take it for granted that we have to teach children about Stranger Danger, but we think that, as adults, we don't need to be concerned. (Well; if you're a guy, you may feel that way. I don't know many women who are cavalier about their personal safety).

Around here, we had a spate of burglaries when various homeowners were away. My husband stopped in one day at the Sheriff's substation to ask what they were doing about it. He was told a) unless there are guns or knives involved, we aren't interested, and b) what do you expect, when you live out in the country? (Honestly? We expected law enforcement to give a rat's ass, but of course, when you're poor and elderly, you don't have the kind of clout that gets you respect from public "servants").

There was one break-in near here where the breakers-and-enterers supposedly broke and climbed through a window - and stepped over the dead body of the homeowner! He was known to have been in ill-health, and presumed to have died from his ailments, but did he? When asked, law enforcement officials refused to say, and we have always wondered if the robbers in fact "helped" the guy to shuffle off this mortal coil.

A number of these crimes occurred after one particular person in the area ran off at the mouth about various neighbors' plans to be away for some period of time. It didn't take us – or anybody else – long to learn not to talk to, or in the presence of, this individual.

When you're meeting someone new, or you're at the feed store, the grocery store, or wherever, and run into an acquaintance, notice if anyone nearby seems unusually interested in your conversation. If a stranger strikes up a conversation with you and asks where you live, feel free to be vague. Actual rudeness may not be necessary, but if it comes to that, I favor an old standby: "None of your business."

Kids make it almost impossible to be entirely secure. If they're very young, they may not understand when you instruct them to be cautious in giving strangers information about home. Even older kids, who do understand, are still kids: wanting to fit in, to impress, they may blurt out information they wouldn't have shared had they thought about it a bit more. And, once one stranger knows something, everybody they talk to knows it.

If you occasionally sell things, try to do it at a flea market. If there isn't one nearby, make arrangements to meet your prospective buyer/s someplace other than your home.

A lot of people living out in the boonies keep guns and/or other weapons for home security. Use your own judgment, but for heaven's sake; if you have firearms, secure them when you leave! One of the things the robbers always help themselves to is guns, If you have a handgun, and the laws in your state allow it, take it with you. Also; don't store the gun and the extra ammunition in the same place. Don't make life any easier for a thief than you can help.

A rancher was telling me one time how crazy and mean people were getting. His place was so big, riders tending cattle or fences often had to spend the night away from the main outfit, so he had set up several "line camps," for them to use. You never locked the door to one of these cabins, because anybody out that far from civilization was liable to be in trouble. People passing through would shelter there for a day or so, and help themselves to beans and flour, etc., as needed. Before leaving, they'd lug in a load of firewood to replace what they'd used, and clean up after themselves. Now, he said, they break out the windows, scatter the beans and flour, and sometimes, even try to burn the place down! I heard this story back in the

68

mid-60s! I can only imagine what things have come to by now.

If you set booby traps for criminals that might break into your home when you're away, and they're injured or killed, be aware that the law will likely regard <u>you</u>, not the crook, as the bad guy. It's not right, it's not fair, but there you are.

Not only human, but animal predators have the protection of the law. A woman once told me about shooting a bear that she caught going after her chickens. I didn't blame her a bit; I think you have a right , and an obligation, to protect what's yours, but I told her to be very careful with whom she shared that story. Increasingly, the law doesn't recognize your right to do any such thing. There are exceptions, in some cases, such as the so-called "stand your ground laws." These have changed the definition of "standing your ground" to mean "pursue and engage, even if told to stand down" (a breathtaking abuse of language, among other things). But, there are exceptions to those laws, as women and minorities have found out the hard way.

Think about what you are prepared to do to protect yourself and your own, and accept that, in a pinch, there may be no other protections except the ones you are willing to undertake on your own.

NOTE: if all this is making you rethink the whole moving-out-into-the-country thing, it shouldn't. Consider how many stories you've heard about city people being assaulted, even murdered, while their neighbors were oblivious or refused to get involved. It's a sad fact that your safety isn't guaranteed anywhere these days. You might as well live where you please, and take the best precautions you can.

CHAPTER 10: Schools and Social Life

<u>Schools</u>

Some rural schools, like some schools in the city, are very good. Some, of course, suck. If you have children, you'll naturally want to check out the schools in your prospective location.

If you'll be near a very small town, understand that they may not have a high school, and instead they bus the kids to the nearest larger town that does have one. In regions where there is often snow and ice, it isn't practical to close school except on days when the roads are clean and dry. For rural students, that means long stretches on the road in inclement weather for a large part of the school year.

Unfortunately, schools now also present the risk of school shootings. I saw on the Internet that someone has invented bullet proof blankets and backpacks to protect kids if there's a shooter in their school. That's nice for the entrepreneurs who come up with these devices, but it's sad to think it's come to that.

If you live in an area that allows home schooling, you may decide to go that route. Check the rules and regs in your state to make sure your lesson plans, tests, etc., meet standardized criteria. That way, your student/s will be able to get into college later, if that's their plan. Schedule get-togethers with other home schooling families wherever possible, so children have an opportunity to socialize.

Some parents home school due to extreme religious, political, and cultural beliefs, wishing to isolate their children from others who believe differently. In my humble opinion, this does the children an enormous disservice. They do not come into your world, but into their own. They deserve every opportunity to find out what and who is out there, and how to make their way among them, if that's where their path leads.

Social Life

The hardest thing, in my opinion, about leaving "civilization" behind is the isolation. In this day of texting, emailing, and social networking, you would think it would be a snap to keep in touch with friends. You'd think physical distance wouldn't be a factor. You might think that, but you might also be wrong.

Our dearest friends lived in the city, 65 miles away. They made the trip out to our place a few times, and always raved about how beautiful it is, how they loved seeing us, etc. When we went to town they insisted on getting together with us for a meal out (alternating whose "treat" it was) or shopping. That lasted about two years. Then they began to be "busy" when we announced that we were coming to town.

Then they stopped calling. They were cordial and seemed glad to talk to us when we called them, but they never called us. Finally, there came a time when we gave up and stopped contacting them, and that was the end of that. Shakespeare, otherwise such an astute judge of human nature apparently got that one wrong: absence does not make the heart grow fonder. Don't be surprised if what you regard as strong ties unravel with distance.

As for making new friends here in our wilderness location, our closest neighbor lived six miles away. He would come see my husband when he wanted help with some chore, vowing to reciprocate, but never doing so. This time, it was we who gave up on him. Another friend, my husband's riding buddy, relocated out of state when his employer moved away.

We don't share the religious and political beliefs of many of the people around here, so we haven't sought to acquaint ourselves with them, nor are they particularly interested in associating with us.

Then, there's always that problem of not knowing who's listening, or who people talk to after they talk to you, as mentioned, so we pretty much keep to ourselves.

To be fair, the last few years that I lived in the city, I had trouble making friends as well. Everybody's life is so busy, it was hard to connect. For instance, the local library had splendid free concerts once a month. In two years, I succeeded in getting friends to attend with me on only two occasions!

One year I had three weavings on exhibit at the county fair. I asked a close friend to go to the fair with me to see the results. She begged off, citing her "crippling fear of crowds," so I went by myself. Each of my pieces placed, winning first, second, and third place ribbons. What fun – and how much fun it would have been to have someone there to share it with. The following year, this same woman attended the fair with another friend whose relative was exhibiting some pieces. (Guess she was over that crowd phobia thingy by then).

I took a knitting class, at which a certain woman always made sure to point out to everyone there (in case they missed it) that, unlike the rest of them, I used only the cheapest yarn. No one told this woman to piss off; that I had as much right to be there – and to my choice of materials, etc., – as anyone else, so I realized that she was speaking for all of them. I stayed long enough to learn a new stitch, and then left the group.

What's the answer? I have no idea. Got no suggestions for you. Shakespeare may have gotten it wrong, but Dylan has it exactly right, when he says, "People are crazy and times are strange."

The thing is; if you have a social circle that is important to you or your loved ones, think twice, about heading off into the wilderness, on the assumption that certain "forever" friends will always be there.

As for your own household, at the very least, there could be regrets, and at worst, outright rebellion. If your spouse or partner doesn't share your dream of living off the land, be careful. Get clear on how far they're willing to go, in every sense, and still stick with you.

Children can be tricky: although they (rightfully) resent being left out of big decisions like leaving home and friends behind, they can also be way more resilient than parents give them credit for. I don't have kids, but I <u>was</u> a kid. I remember the resentment I felt when my parents would try to "shield" me from some big upheaval until it was too late to hide the fact that there were going to be BIG CHANGES.

By the same token, I hate the way that modern parents seem to let the kids run their lives. I want to scream when one of those commercials comes on where the hapless parents decide what car, or what phone service, or whatever, to buy based on input on the part of their child. If the children are at least school age, a family council may be appropriate, but the grown-ups need to be the grown-ups.

I can't tell you if it would be a good idea to uproot your family and move them out to the boondocks. Some people – children and adults – are unable to feel at home away from the hustle and bustle of city life. Neal Diamond even wrote a song about what he calls the "beautiful noise" of the city. Frankly, I don't think it's so beautiful. Noise pollution is a big part of the stress of living in a city. You may get used to it, but that doesn't mean it's somehow become good for you.

Anyway; the right thing to do is never going to be the same for everyone. Do the best you can.

CHAPTER 11: Recreation

<u>Happy Trails</u>

There's plenty to do out in the back of beyond. Here, for instance, if you like to ride it seems like you can take a different trail every day. Certainly, it's not necessary to take the same trail often enough to become bored with it. If horseback riding isn't to your taste, there's hiking, mountain biking, trail biking, and ATVs.

One day as I was headed out to the highway, I passed a group of about two dozen ATV-ers heading in. Families, for the most part, moms, dads, and kids, with picnic coolers, eager to get out and have an adventure. It looked like fun. (Of course, one hopes they stayed on the trails and that they knew better than to harass livestock and wildlife).

As I said, our preferences ran to horses. Riding is one of those activities, like scuba diving, that is best done with a buddy, and I don't mean your horse, although I hope you have a great bond with him or her. Even the best-natured, calmest horse, confronted with a frightening situation can panic, and, as a prey animal, their hardwired first reaction is to bolt and run away. A well-trained horse may not run far, and a horse that trusts you may calm down and again take direction from you, but if you come out of that saddle in the meantime, well; it's just a good idea to ride in the company of another human. Failing that, take your cell phone with you (we get a good signal, even out here). Keep it on you, not in one of those cute little pouches you can get for your saddle. That way, if you find yourself watching your horse heading for home, your phone will be with <u>you</u>. Do that, and make sure somebody knows approximately where you'll be going and when you expect to be back, and enjoy your ride.

When you leave the home place to see what there is to see, don't have so much fun that you forget to stay alert. Things to watch out for definitely include livestock. Most cattle will watch you long enough to determine that a) you didn't bring hay, and b) you aren't there to round them up. After that, they lose interest pretty quickly. Sometimes, though, a cow with a very young calf will assume you're a threat to her baby, whether you are or not, and will take steps to protect her little one.

My husband was out riding his horse, Tazha, one day, and had three of the dogs with him. He passed a group of cows at what he felt was a comfortable distance, but one mama decided he was dangerous, and she needed to let him know he wasn't welcome. She charged at horse and rider for a few paces and then stopped, and stood there snorting and tossing her head in case they were too dim to take the hint. She had the kind of horns that angle out and straight up, so if she lowered her head and then brought it up under the horse, an honest-to-god tragedy was sure to follow. The dogs stood there staring at her, uneasy, but too well-mannered to chase her without a signal from their human, who was undecided whether he needed help with the old biddy. (One of those cases where one has to balance the law with personal safety...). Tazha was letting his rider know he wanted to turn tail and book, but Benjamin kept him facing the old gal, on the theory that if they were looking at her, she might be less likely to continue her attack.

Unfortunately, she ran at them again, getting too close for Benjamin's comfort, and Tazha was REALLY wanting to turn and put some distance between them and that cow, such that Benjamin wasn't real sure he could keep control of his mount.

At that point, one of the dogs realized that this was a serious deal, and that old cow meant to hurt her dad. (She wasn't that fond of Tazha)! She skinned her lips back until it looked like her whole head was full of <u>teeth</u>, and faced down that cow.

The cow, seeing that here was a real, as opposed to a potential, threat, said, "Okay; maybe not." She backed down and the dog held her ground long enough to give horse, rider, and other dogs time to put a safe distance between themselves and the over-protective mama.

Usually, as I said, livestock is going to check you out enough to satisfy their curiosity. After that, they'll go their way and let you go yours. Wildlife will do the same thing, covertly. I can't tell you how many times I've caught a glimpse of a coyote or a javelina headed away from me. I know very well they've been watching, no doubt having spotted me long before I spotted them. The coyotes know the range of our guns – and, seemingly, which guns we're carrying, even if we haven't fired them – and they stay just out of range! We've never killed a coyote, but we've fired plenty of warning shots at them, and we want them to fear us. (Arizonans are encouraged to make a clamor when there are coyotes: these animals are bold and will keep encroaching until you make the boundaries clear to them). They skulk around and kill our barn cats, sometimes in broad daylight. It's really hard to accept that they will take one of the cats, when the place is lousy with cottontails and jackrabbits, along with smaller rodents. Ultimately the only way to protect your pets, not to mention small children, is keep them in the house, and to supervise them when they're outside.

Javelinas are new to this area in recent years. They're a desert species, and never used to come up to these altitudes, where it snows. There are a couple of reasons I don't like seeing the javelinas here. One; they can be aggressive, and they can kill your dogs, and you, too. They have wicked tusks that they can use to slash your legs out from under you. If they get you down, it could be over for you real quick. I've had them chase my dogs when we're out walking. Fortunately, it's been easy enough to scare them off and get my dogs to come back by firing a warning shot into the ground, but seeing them makes me uneasy. As if their presence weren't bad enough, javelina is a delicacy to the mountain lion. If you're a horse person, lion's one of the last critters you want moving into the neighborhood.

We're also seeing roadrunners, which are kind of neat, and I enjoy watching them. Roadrunners' diet includes rattlesnakes, and for my money, they can have 'em all. So far, I've never been confronted by a rattler when I was out hiking or riding. I asked a horse trainer friend if I should acquire a set of rattles and use them to desensitize our horses, so they won't freak out if they ever hear the real deal. She said in her experience, they don't freak out. They go hyper-alert, but you can safely, and slowly, move them away from the snake without a wreck or a runaway. (Of course, all horses, like all people, are different, and I wouldn't take anything for granted about their reaction to something they know – or think – can hurt them).

If you're hiking, the conventional wisdom is that you don't put your foot or hand any place where you can't see what might be waiting there. If you do find yourself facing a snake and he's rattling, that's his way of saying, "Get away from me!" In that case, do that very thing, but be sure to move slowly and carefully. I was out walking one morning and saw a big bull snake in my path. (They will sometimes shake their tails at you; they don't have rattles, but they mimic the behavior to scare you off). I backed carefully away, keeping my eyes on him, and he lay where he was, keeping his eyes on me. When I was fifty feet or so away, I turned around and went a few more steps. When I looked back, he was gone.

A new threat out here is the green mohave rattlesnake. Our vet said, unlike the rattlers we've always had around here, the green mohave will chase you. With one of those, you don't worry about not making any fast moves: you want all the speed you can muster!

Rattlesnakes live all over the U.S., unless it's still true that they don't live east of the Cascades in Washington State. I last heard that in the nineties, and with all the strange weather, etc., it wouldn't surprise me to find they've moved in there, too.

If you live in the South, there are also water moccasins and cottonmouths that can get you. (And, of course, there are also the boa constrictors whose idiot owners have dumped them or let them escape). If that's not enough, there are the gators. Glad I don't live in those parts; I have enough to deal with right where I am. If you do live in one of those areas, be vigilant for yourself and your loved ones, including pets.

My friend has stopped letting his cats out to patrol the property; he's tired of losing them. I understand that, but I don't look forward to the influx of vermin that's sure to come. A retired mechanic, he has often refused to work on vehicles that belonged to people who don't like and don't have cats. Those cars and trucks can quickly be trashed by rodents. The darn things tear up upholstery for nesting material, chew up wiring, and pee and poop on everything they can reach – meaning; pretty much everything. There was a rodent caught about forty miles from here, found to carry the deadly hanta virus. That's way too close for comfort, even putting aside the aesthetics of trying to work on somebody's old ride that's been fouled.

I have looked for alternatives to poison and traps, which we refuse to use for several reasons. There are mouse/rat repellents that seem to depend on mint and/or other aromatic oils. I keep peppermint oil on hand. I make up a peppermint hydrosol (a fancy way of describing water with a few drops of essential oil in it), which I keep in a spray bottle. I use that to treat the doorways where spiders and mice are likely to come into the house.

Before that, one mouse did get in, and made him/herself at home for several nerve-wracking nights. I would lie in bed, just starting to fall asleep and hear the little devil knock something over on one of my counters! Of course, that would make sleep unthinkable, until the next time I started to doze off in spite of myself, and the same thing would happen.

One of my dogs would happily have made short work of the rodent, but that was another fear: had he killed the thing, he'd have brought it to bed. Since I share that bed with his sister and him, I preferred that he not do that! I finally set a trap baited with peanut butter in the silverware drawer, which I left slightly open. I chose this as a place I could set a trap without one of my dogs getting into it. The next morning, sure enough, the critter was history. I take no pleasure in killing even a mouse, but neither do I want them making themselves at home in <u>my</u> home!

We have yellow jackets, too; also called "mud daubers." These wasps are quite a problem some summers, but at least, in my experience, they aren't aggressive. The problem comes when they get into the house and make their mud nests in the cupboards, even in the sleeves of coats in the closets! I caught a few in wasp traps that I put up, but not enough (meaning, not all of them)! I plan to put up some of those fake nests you see in some of the seed catalogs. The theory is that the wasps will see that this is someone else's territory, and move on. We'll see.

(As I was putting the finishing touches on this manuscript, I decided to set up my peg loom for a new project. I was outraged to find some of the holes occluded with mud! When I cleaned them out, there was also, let's just say, moist stuff...ick. Quickly on the heels of that discovery, I observed one of the vile things going behind my bookcase, and found two more nests stuck to the pages of two books! Grrr: <u>Death</u> to mud daubers)!

CONCLUSION

Allow me to share a page from one of my journal entries on one winter's day:

"Battened down for another snow storm. B went into town for a load of water today, in case we can't get out for awhile. Then he came home and cut and split firewood while I loaded it into the trailer.

"Dragged as much wood into the house as I could and then filled the wood cart and parked it in the shed out of the weather. Helped B tarp the wood in the wood trailer.

"Supposed to start snowing tonight sometime after midnight and bring another 6-8 inches, so another 4-5 days of mud after that. Mud on the floor, mud in my bed(!), mud gooped up on my muck boots till it feels like each foot weighs 40 pounds.

"I don't believe in hell, but I told B if there is one, it's not fiery: it's muddy.

"(The upside is, not only will the rain tanks be full, but we should have some decent grass in the spring, so we'll spend less on hay. I'll try to be glad about that when I'm dealing with the mess)."

-/-/-

If you're still with me, I guess I haven't managed to scare you too much. Living off grid, and way off the beaten path, is like living anywhere: it has its good points and its bad points. I love seeing my horses ramble around the place, going about their horsey business. I love seeing my dogs, who are normally pretty sedentary, racing around like kids when school's out, when I take them for their daily "walk" without leaving home. I love watching the weather; there's a big sky out here, and it's constantly changing; there are rainbows and sunsets and dawns to delight the heart. The stars are spectacular – how many city people get to <u>see</u> the stars now, without going to a planitarium or watching a space program on TV?

You become super-efficient living out here, or you don't make it. When it's a 20-mile round trip to the nearest town, you plan. Making one run in to check the mail, and another to go to the library, and another to see a friend, etc., doesn't make sense out here (of course, it doesn't really make sense if you live in the city, either). If you're used to being spontaneous, you will have to accept a greater level of discipline about managing your time. That, of course, isn't necessarily a bad thing.

I hope that, whether you decide to go off grid or not, you have learned a few helpful things in reading this little book. I hope, if you decide to go for it and live your dream, you never look back.

RESOURCES

Many of these were unavailable when we were starting out. If you aren't online, take advantage of the free public computers and/or wifi at your local library. (As always, use public wifi for research only, not for shopping, banking, or any other activity that might make your personal information available to tech-savvy criminals).

Hydroponics:

abgrowingsupplies.com

If you live in or near Prescott, Arizona, this is a great place to learn about the subject. Ask when they're going to do another seminar.

Tiny houses:

Tinyhousedesign.com

The tiny house movement is picking up steam in this country, but make sure whatever house you want to build meets "code" for where you'll be building it.

Straw bale building:

strawbale.com

Earthships:

earthship.com

Solar Lanterns:

dlite.com

luminaid.com

Adopting wild horses and/or burros:

blm.gov

Find out about online adoption and auctions in your area. The website also has lots of info about wildhorses and burros:

Adopting domestic horses, burros, and other animals:

donkeyrescue.org

Peaceful Valley Donkey Rescue. They're based in California, but have satellite locations in some other states. They literally wrote the book about donkeys; you can buy a copy, along with other items, at their website.

Animal Rescues and Shelters:

Websites? Far too many!

NOTE: there are rescues for all sizes and kinds of animals these days. Some animals are surrendered by owners who can't afford to keep them, others are abandoned, and still others are seized from abuse and neglect situations. If you have room in your heart and your life for a needy animal, please look for these organizations in your area. They will check you out along with the proposed accommodations for your animal/s. Expect to pay an adoption fee to a rescue or to the BLM: these help defray their expenses, and are much cheaper than you would pay a breeder to purchase one of their animals, plus you will be saving a life, or lives.

Horse training:

Parelli.com

Pat and Linda Parelli aren't the only humane horse trainers, but they promote the idea of building a great relationship with your horse, where many others are all about training your horse and trading him/her for the next one. Animals are not expendable, so I like the Parellis.

Fermentation/cultured food preparation:

Wildfermentation.com

Culturedfoodlife.com

Sustainability, resilience, permaculture:

resilientcommunities.org

thrivingresilience.org

permaculture.org

permacultureprinciples.com

Country living:

backwoodshome.com

lehmans.com

Lehmans has the "water glass" mentioned above, along with many non-electric items you may need.

Farming with horses, mules, and oxen:

ruralheritage.com

Keeping chickens:

backyardchicken.com

Solar refrigerators:

sundanzer.com

Makers of solar-powered refrigerators and freezers. There are others, as well, but we saw one of these units at a sustainability exhibition and liked it. BTW: these are chest-type units, rather than uprights. This because, of course, heat rises, and the upright design you're accustomed to is undoubtedly handier, but not energy-efficient....

-/-/-

NOTE: Enjoy these and any other information sources you discover, but remember: nobody knows it all, online or in person. Listen to your intuition. If you find yourself being pressured to accept anything at face value, if you are being discouraged from checking it out, beware. An old racetracker taught me long ago, "If anyone tells you, 'I know everything there is to know about horses,' run: he'll get you and/or your horse hurt or killed." The same goes for a lot of self-styled "experts," so question "authority".

www.ingramcontent.com/pod-product-compliance
Lightning Source LLC
Chambersburg PA
CBHW071224280526
45787CB00002B/791